Let's learn about Gur

Happy Gurpurab

Gurkiran Sandhu

Gurpurab is the Sikh festival celebrated when it is birthday of any of the 10 Sikh Gurus. Gurpurab is also an occasion when death's of Gurus is observed. These Gurus were responsible for shaping the beliefs of the Sikhs.

Gurpurab is an occasion for celebration and prayer among the Sikhs. Gurpurab is celebrated with great enthusiasm by Sikhs all over the world.

Guru Nanak Dev Ji

Guru Nanak Gurpurab, also known as Guru Nanak Jayanti, celebrates the birth of the first Sikh Guru, Guru Nanak Dev Ji. This is one of the most sacred festivals in Sikhism.

The celebrations usually start with Prabhat Pheris. Prabhat Pheris are early morning processions that begin at the Gurudwara and proceed around the localities singing hymns.

Heads are covered during Prabhat Pheris and kids enjoy Prabhat Pheris as much as adults do.

Usually, two days before the birthday, Akhand Path is held in the Gurdwaras.

Akhand paath is the continuous nonstop recitation of all the verses in the Guru Granth Sahib from the beginning to the end, in 31 Ragas as specified, in all 1430 pages, lasting more than 48 hours by a team of readers.

The day prior to the birthday, a procession, referred to as Nagar keertan, is organized. Nagar keertan is a Sikh custom involving the processional singing of holy hymns throughout a community.

Traditionally, the procession is led by the saffron-robed Panj Piare. Panj Piare are the five beloved of the Guru. Panj Piare are followed by the Guru Granth Sahib, and the holy Sikh scripture—which is placed on a float.

In addition, there are brass bands playing different tunes and 'Gatka' teams display their swordsmanship through various martial arts and as mock battles using traditional weapons.

The path of Nagar Keertan is covered with banners and gates decorated flags and flowers, for this special occasion.

On the day of the Gurpurab, the celebrations start early in the morning at about 4 to 5 am. This time of the day is referred to as 'Amrit Vela'.

The day begins with the singing of Asa-di-Var. Asa-di-Var are defined as the morning hymns.

Asa-di-Var is followed by any combination of Katha (exposition of the scripture) and Keertan (hymns from the Sikh scriptures), in the praise of the Guru.

Following Katha/Keertan is the Langar, a special community lunch, which is arranged at the Gurdwaras by volunteers.

The idea behind langar or the free communal lunch is that everyone, irrespective of caste, class or creed, should be offered food in the spirit of seva (service) and bhakti (devotion).

Night Prayer sessions are also held in some Gurdwaras on Gurpurab. Night prayers start when Rehras Saheb(evening prayer) is recited and is followed by Keertan till late at night.

The worshipers begin singing Gurbani at about 1:20 am at night, which is the actual time of birth of Guru Nanak and the celebrations culminate at around 2 am.

Happy
Guru Gobind Singh Ji's
Jayanti..!!

Guru Gobind Singh, the tenth Guru's Birthday generally falls in December or January. The celebrations are similar to those of Guru Nanak's birthday, namely Akhand Paath, procession and Keertan, Katha, and Langar.

Guru Arjun Dev sitting in boiling water

The martyrdom anniversary of Guru Arjan Dev Ji, the fifth Guru, falls in May or June, the hottest months in India. He was tortured to death under the orders of Mughal Emperor, Jahangir, at Lahore on 25 May 1606.

The occasion consists of Keertan, Katha and Langar in the Gurdwara. Because of summer heat, chilled sweetened drink made from milk, sugar, essence and water, called "chhabeel" is freely distributed in Gurdwaras to everybody irrespective of their religious beliefs.

Look for other interesting Sikh Books on Amazon·com

Let's learn about Bandi Chhor Divas, Kids!

Gurkiran Sandhu

Let's learn about Hola Mohala, Kids!

Gurkiran Sandhu

Let's learn about Vaisakhi, Kids!

Gurkiran Sandhu

Let's learn about Lohri, Kids!

Gurkiran Sandhu

Let's learn about Gurpurab, Kids!
Gurkiran Sandhu

Made in the USA
Middletown, DE
02 November 2021

51564280R00015